BRAIN QUEST

LEARN to WRITE

TRACING, SHAPES, AND MORE

T0015770

workman

• New York •

This book belongs to:

FIRST NAME

LAST NAME

ISBN 978-1-5235-1599-8

Design by Daniella Graner, Keirsten Geise, and John Passineau
Illustrations by Matthew Scott
Edited by Alisha Zucker

Workman books are available at special discounts when purchased in bulk for premiums and sales promotions as well as for fundraising or educational use. Special editions or book excerpts can also be created to specification. For details, please contact special.markets@hbgusa.com.

Workman Publishing Co., Inc., a subsidiary of Hachette Book Group, Inc.
1290 Avenue of the Americas
New York, NY 10104

workman.com

Distributed in Europe by Hachette Livre, 58 rue Jean Bleuzen, 92 178 Vanves Cedex, France.

Distributed in the United Kingdom by Hachette Book Group, UK, Carmelite House, 50 Victoria Embankment, London EC4Y 0DZ.

Printed in Canada on responsibly sourced paper.

First printing July 2023

10 9 8 7 6 5 4 3 2 1

DEAR PARENTS AND CAREGIVERS,

At Brain Quest we believe learning is an adventure, a quest for knowledge. We're delighted to partner with you and your child as they begin their exciting journey exploring the fundamentals of writing.

LEARN TO WRITE: PEN CONTROL, TRACING, SHAPES, AND MORE provides lots of opportunities for your child to practice fundamental penmanship skills and prepares them for a lifetime of writing. Learning to draw lines, curves, and shapes is an important first step toward writing letters and numbers.

Tips for Using This Book:

Follow your child's lead. Let them decide how much writing to do in one sitting.

Be hands on. Guide your child to trace the large red example lines with their fingers and the blue dashed lines with their pencils.

Offer support. Read the directions aloud. Model how to trace the big numbers with your finger or hold the pencil correctly as needed.

Praise their effort. Compliment your learner's effort and persistence.

Celebrate success! Use stickers from the back of the book to reward effort and success, and cut out the certificate to mark your child's accomplishment.

Enjoy this first step as your child learns to write!

Hold the pencil with the thumb and index fingers. Rest the pencil on the middle finger.

—The editors of Brain Quest

Horizontal Lines

Trace the horizontal line with your finger.

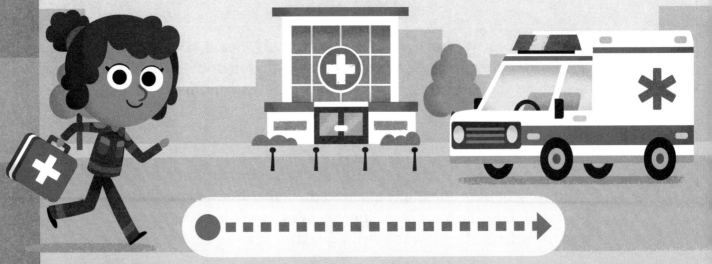

Trace each line. Start at the **red** dot.

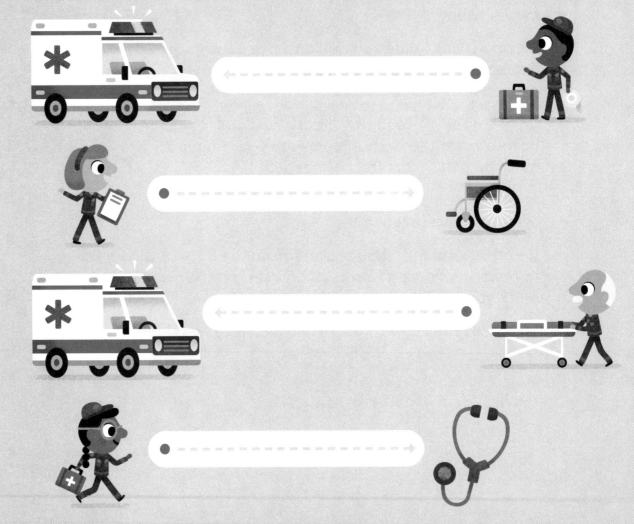

Draw each line. Start at the red dot.

Trace the lines to help the
ambulance get to the hospital.

Horizontal Lines

Trace the horizontal line with your finger.

Trace each line. Start at the **red** dot.

Draw each line. Start at the red dot.

Trace the lines on the police car.

Vertical Lines

Trace the vertical line with your finger.

Trace each line. Start at the red dot.

Draw each line. Start at the red dot.

Trace the lines on the boat and the lighthouse.

Vertical Lines

Trace the vertical line with your finger.

Draw each line. Start at the **red** dot.

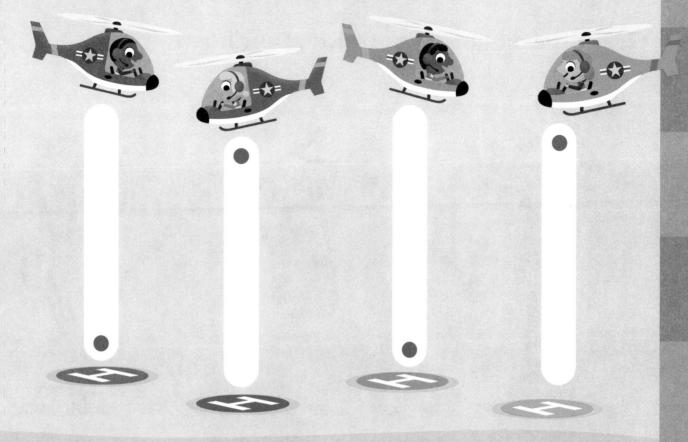

Trace the lines in the picture.

Diagonal Lines

Trace the diagonal lines with your finger.

Trace each line. Start at the **red dot.**

Draw each line. Start at the **red** dot.

Draw lines to connect the firefighters to the matching boots.

PLACE STICKER HERE

Brain Quest Learn to Write: Pen Control, Tracing, Shapes, and More

Diagonal Lines

Trace the diagonal lines
with your finger.

Trace each line. Start at the red dot.

Draw each line. Start at the **red** dot.

Trace the lines on the trails.

PLACE STICKER HERE

Let's Review

Trace the lines in the picture.

PLACE STICKER HERE

Helpers at Work

Draw lines to help the park ranger get back to her truck.

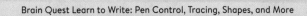

Draw a line to connect each vehicle to the matching helper.

Brain Quest Learn to Write: Pen Control, Tracing, Shapes, and More

Zigzags

Trace the zigzags with your finger.

Trace each zigzag. Start at the red dot.

Draw each zigzag. Start at the **red** dot.

Trace the zigzags.

PLACE STICKER HERE

Zigzags

Trace the **zigzags** with your finger.

Trace each zigzag. Start at the **red** dot.

Draw each zigzag. Start at the **red** dot.

Trace the zigzags.

PLACE STICKER HERE

Brain Quest Learn to Write: Pen Control, Tracing, Shapes, and More

Zigzags

Trace the zigzag with your finger.

Trace each zigzag. Start at the red dot.

Draw each zigzag. Start at the **red dot.**

Trace the zigzags.

So Many Zigzags

Trace the zigzags.

Trace the zigzags to help the clown get back to the circus.

Let's Review

Trace the lines in the picture.

Curved Lines

Trace the curved line with your finger.

Trace each line. Start at the **red** dot.

Draw each line. Start at the **red** dot.

Trace the curved lines.

PLACE
STICKER HERE

Curved Lines

Trace the **curved line** with your finger.

Trace each line. Start at the **red** dot.

Trace the curved lines.

Curved Lines

Trace the curved line with your finger.

Trace each line. Start at the **red** dot.

Draw each line. Start at the **red** dot.

Trace the curved lines.

Curved Lines

Trace the curved line with your finger.

Trace each line. Start at the **red** dot.

Draw each line. Start at the **red** dot.

Trace the curved lines.

Let's Review

Draw the lines on the
roller coaster.

Go-Carts Go

Trace the path to connect the driver with the flag.

Trace the lines on the go-cart track.

Park Paths

Draw lines to show the children's paths through the amusement park.

Ride Time!

Trace the lines in the picture.

Fun and Games

Trace the lines in the amusement park.

Squares

Trace the square with your finger.

Trace each square. Start at the red dot.

Draw squares to add windows. Start at the **red** dot.

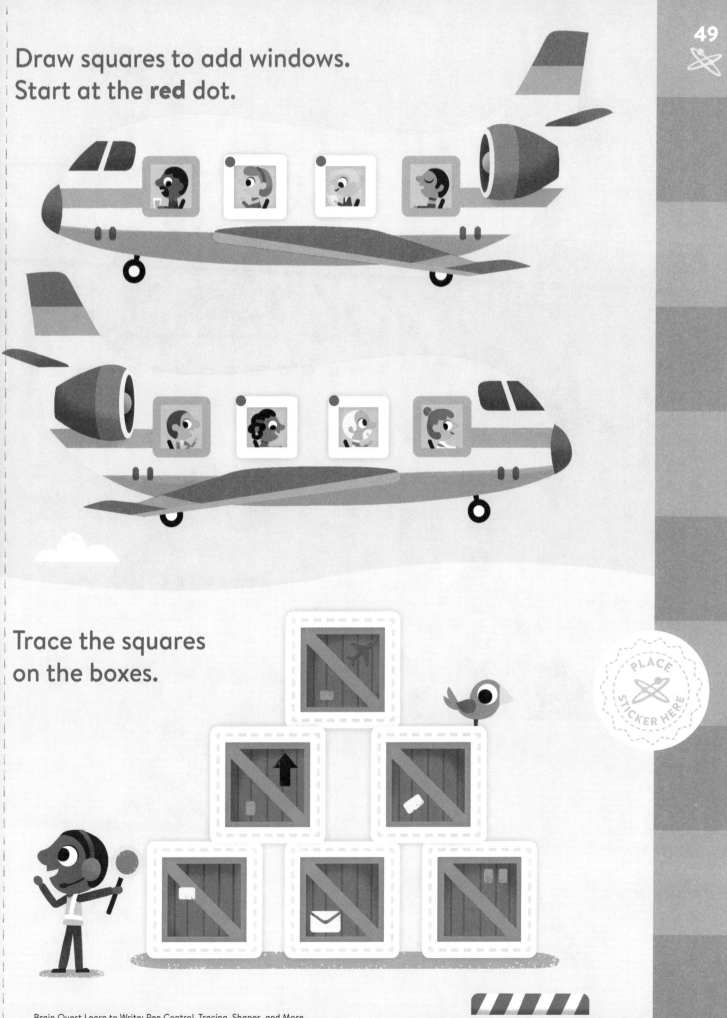

Trace the squares on the boxes.

Triangles

Trace the triangle with your finger.

Trace each triangle. Start at the **red** dot.

Draw each triangle. Start at the **red** dot.

Trace the triangles.

PLACE STICKER HERE

Rectangles

Trace the rectangle with your finger.

Trace each rectangle. Start at the **red** dot.

Draw each rectangle. Start at the red dot.

Trace the rectangles.

PLACE STICKER HERE

Rectangles

Trace the **rectangle** with your finger.

Trace each rectangle. Start at the **red** dot.

Draw each rectangle. Start at the **red** dot.

Trace the rectangles.

PLACE STICKER HERE

Let's Review

Trace the shapes.

Circles

Trace the circle with your finger.

Trace each circle. Start at the **red** dot.

Draw circles around the planets. Start at the **red** dot.

Draw circles on the moon.

PLACE STICKER HERE

Ovals

Trace the oval with your finger.

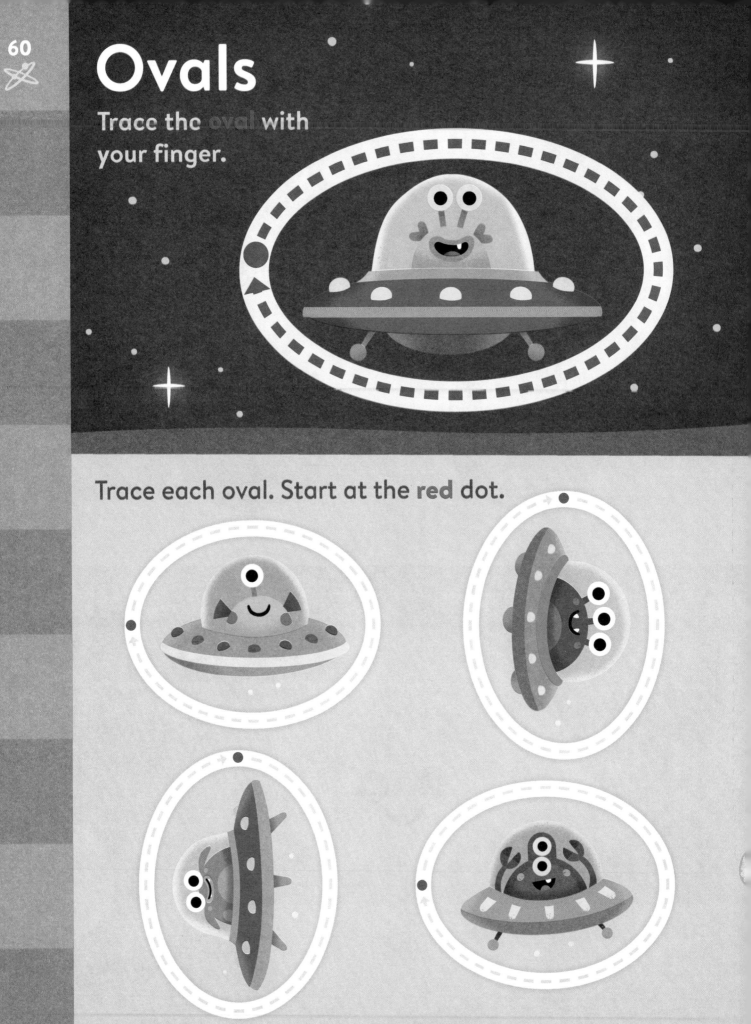

Trace each oval. Start at the **red dot**.

Draw ovals around the spaceships. Start at the **red** dot.

Draw ovals around the spaceships.

Hearts

Trace the heart with your finger.

Trace each heart. Start at the **red** dot.

Draw hearts on the aliens' shirts. Start at the **red** dot.

Draw a heart on this friendship flag.

PLACE STICKER HERE

Stars

Trace the **star** with your finger.

Trace each star. Start at the red dot.

Draw each star. Start at the red dot.

Trace the star. Then draw more stars in space.

PLACE
STICKER HERE

Let's Review

Trace the shapes in outer space.

Beach Paths

Draw the paths on the beach.

Biking Home

Draw the bikers' paths home.
Trace the shapes they see
on the way.

All the Shapes

Trace the **square**. Then draw your own.

Trace the **rectangle**. Then draw your own.

Trace the **triangle**. Then draw your own.

Trace the **circle**. Then draw your own.

Trace the **oval**. Then draw your own.

Trace the **heart**. Then draw your own.

Trace the **star**. Then draw your own.

Patterns

Draw the next shape in the pattern.

Draw your own shape pattern here.

Shape Matching

Draw lines to match the shapes.

Mazes

Help the astronaut get back to her space shuttle.

Help the alien get back to his home planet.

Best Shape Awards

Draw your best of each shape on the awards.
Circle your favorite!

CONGRATULATIONS!

Write your name here:

COMPLETED

LEARN to WRiTE

PEN CONTROL

PLACE HERE STICKER

Trace the lines and shapes. Color the stickers!